PLESIOSAURUS

THE SWIMMING REPTILE

by

Elizabeth J. Sandell

DINOSAUR DISCOVERY ERA

Bancroft-Sage Publishing

601 Elkcam Circle, Suite C-7, Box 355, Marco, FL 33969

Exclusive distributor

ENCYCLOPAEDIA BRITANNICA EDUCATIONAL CORPORATION

TRAINING & DEVELOPMENT

310 South Michigan Avenue Chicago, IL 60604

LIBRARY OF CONGRESS CATALOGING IN PUBLICATION DATA

Sandell, Elizabeth J.
 Plesiosaurus: the swimming reptile.

 (Dinosaur discovery era)
 SUMMARY: An introduction to the physical characteristics, habits, and natural environment of the dinosaur-like, sea reptile known as plesiosaurus.
 1. Plesiosaurus--Juvenile literature. (1. Plesiosaurus. 2. Reptiles. 3. Dinosaurs.) I. Oelerich, Marjorie L. II. Schroeder, Howard. III. Vista III Design. IV. Title. V. Series.
 QE862.P4S26   1988   567.9'3   88-962
 ISBN 0-944280-04-8 (lib. bdg.)
 ISBN 0-944280-10-2 (pbk. bdg.)

International Standard Book Number:	**Library of Congress Catalog Card Number:**
Library Binding 0-944280-04-8	88-962
Paperback Binding 0-944280-10-2	

SPECIAL THANKS FOR THEIR HELP AND COOPERATION TO:
Mary R. Carman, Paleontology Collection Manager
Field Museum of Natural History
Chicago, Illinois

Copyright 1988 by Bancroft-Sage Productions and Publishing. All rights reserved. No part of this book may be reproduced in any form without written permission from the publisher, except for brief passages included in a review. Printed in the United States of America.

PLESIOSAURUS
THE SWIMMING REPTILE

AUTHOR
Elizabeth J. Sandell

dedicated to Meghan Deery

EDITED BY
Marjorie L. Oelerich, Ph.D.
Professor of Early Childhood and Elementary Education
Mankato State University

Howard Schroeder, Ph.D.
Professor of Reading and Language Arts
Dept. of Curriculum and Instruction
Mankato State University
Mankato, MN

ILLUSTRATED BY
Vista III Design

BANCROFT-SAGE PUBLISHING
112 Marshall St., Box 1968, Mankato, MN 56001-1968 U.S.A.

INTRODUCTION: MYCHAL VISITS MR. BONES' MUSEUM

Barnum Brown was so well-known for the fossils he found that people called him "Mr. Bones." The fossils that Mr. Bones found were from leaves, shells, bones, teeth, eggs, skin, fur, and footprints. Fossils are the remains of plants and animals that lived thousands of years ago and were buried in mud and sand.

"Mr. Bones" was a paleontologist who brought all kinds of fossils to the American Museum of Natural History in New York City, New York (USA). He found them as far away as the Red Deer River near Content, Alberta (Canada). He also found some near Como Bluff, Wyoming (USA).

Mychal saw Mr. Bones' fossils when he went to the American Museum of Natural History with his father. This building has the greatest number of dinosaur fossils in the world. Dinosaurs were large animals that lived on the earth a long time ago.

Mychal and his father stopped to talk to the museum guide. The guide knew all about the exhibits in the museum.

"I've never seen so many dinosaur bones all in one place!" Mychal told the guide.

"Well, Mychal," the guide said, "the museum has lots of other fossils, too, besides the bones of dinosaurs. We also have *Mosasaurus, Pterodactylus, Crocodilians,* and *Plesiosaurus.*

"These animals are also in the exhibits in the museum," the guide explained. "Let's look at a few, so you will know about some animals other than dinosaurs."

He led Mychal and his father into another exhibit room, and there was a fossilized *Plesiosaurus.* The guide told them that *Plesiosaurus* was known as a swimming reptile. He told how the bones of this creature were found more than 160 years ago.

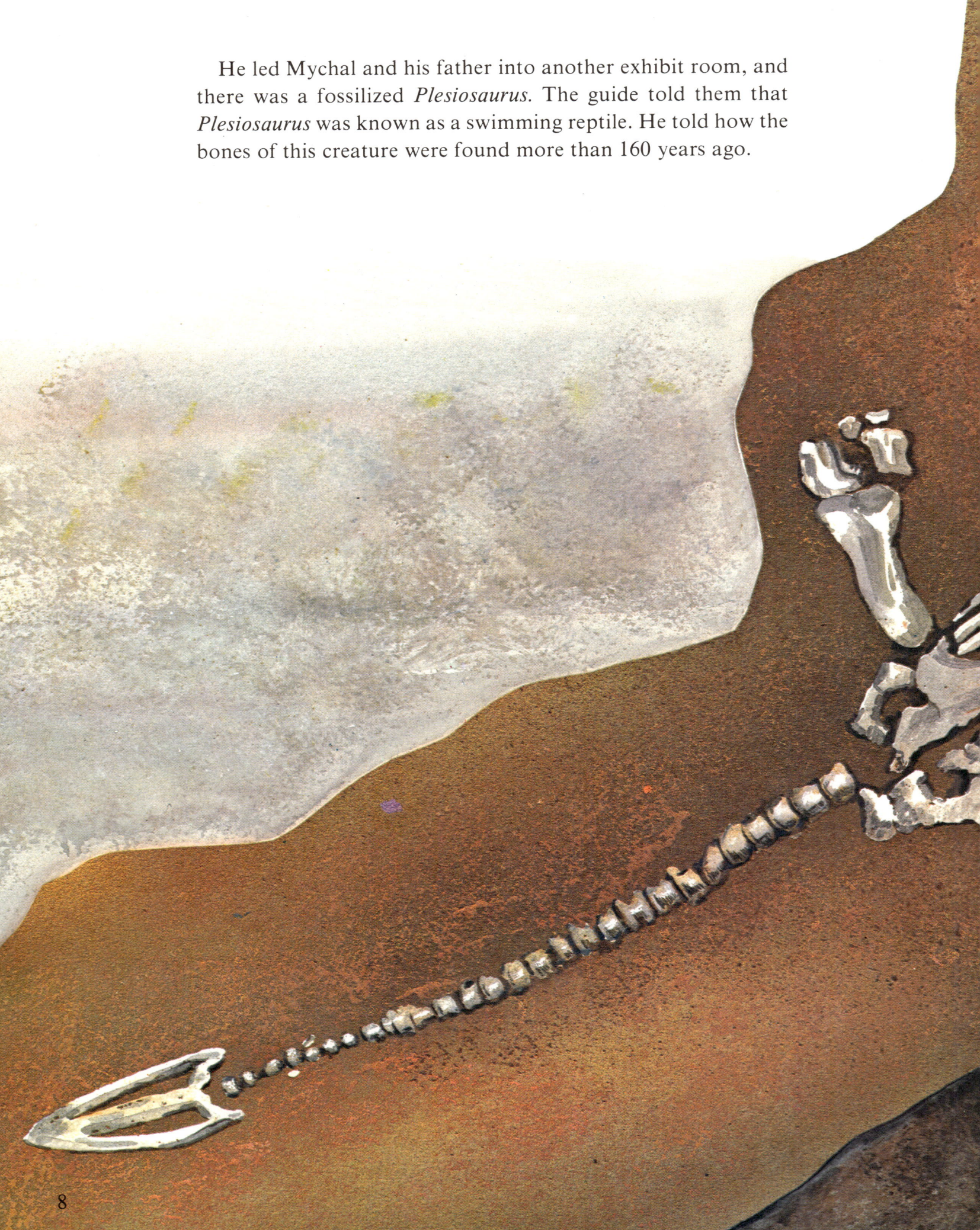

CHAPTER 1: DISCOVERING PLESIOSAURUS

In the 1800's, in a little town on the south seacoast of England (Europe), people could buy fossils from eleven-year-old Mary Anning. She would gather fossils on the beach and along the high cliffs.

In 1821, Mary found a fossil of a large sea reptile with a short and wide body, four large flippers instead of legs, and a very long neck. Henry De la Beche, a scientist, called it *Plesiosaurus* (ple´ se uh sor´ uhs). This word means "nearly like a lizard."

Three years later, Mary found another *Plesiosaurus* fossil with an even longer neck.

DINOSAURS AND REPTILES

Scientists once thought that *Plesiosaurus* was related to the dinosaurs. *Plesiosaurus* lived during the same time. Its body was shaped like a barrel, as were the bodies of some dinosaurs.

However, we now know that *Plesiosaurus* was not a dinosaur. The legs of *Plesiosaurus* were different than those of a dinosaur. *Plesiosaurus* had flippers attached to the sides of its body. A dinosaur had legs under its body.

Also, *Plesiosaurus* moved differently. The flippers caused it to crawl on its stomach when it was on land. These flippers helped it to swim in water.

Plesiosaurus did not have joints in its legs. A dinosaur did have joints, which helped it to walk. The joints (which were like knees) in the back legs of the dinosaur pointed forward. The joints in its front legs pointed backward.

Plesiosaurus was really a reptile instead of a dinosaur.

FAMILY NAMES

Plesiosaur was the name for a group of swimming reptiles that lived thousands of years ago. These reptiles ate fish and swam with flippers.

There were two groups of *plesiosaurs.*

One group was called *plesiosauroids* (ple´ se uh sor´ oids). They had long snake-like necks, small heads, and bodies shaped like barrels. They swam near the top of the sea so they could breathe air. The animals called *Plesiosaurus* and *Elasmosaurus* (i laz´ muh sor´ uhs) were in this group.

The other group was called *pliosauroids* (pli´ uh sor´ oids). They had short necks, large heads, and bodies like a whale. They dived down into the sea to catch fish.

CHAPTER 2: PLESIOSAURUS SWAM IN THE SEAS

When *Plesiosaurus* lived so many years ago, the weather was very warm and pleasant. On the land, there were ferns, grass, and other plants. There were also many kinds of trees, such as palm, willow, walnut, oak, cycad, and sweet gum.

Shallow seas covered much of North America and Europe. The land might have looked like this map.

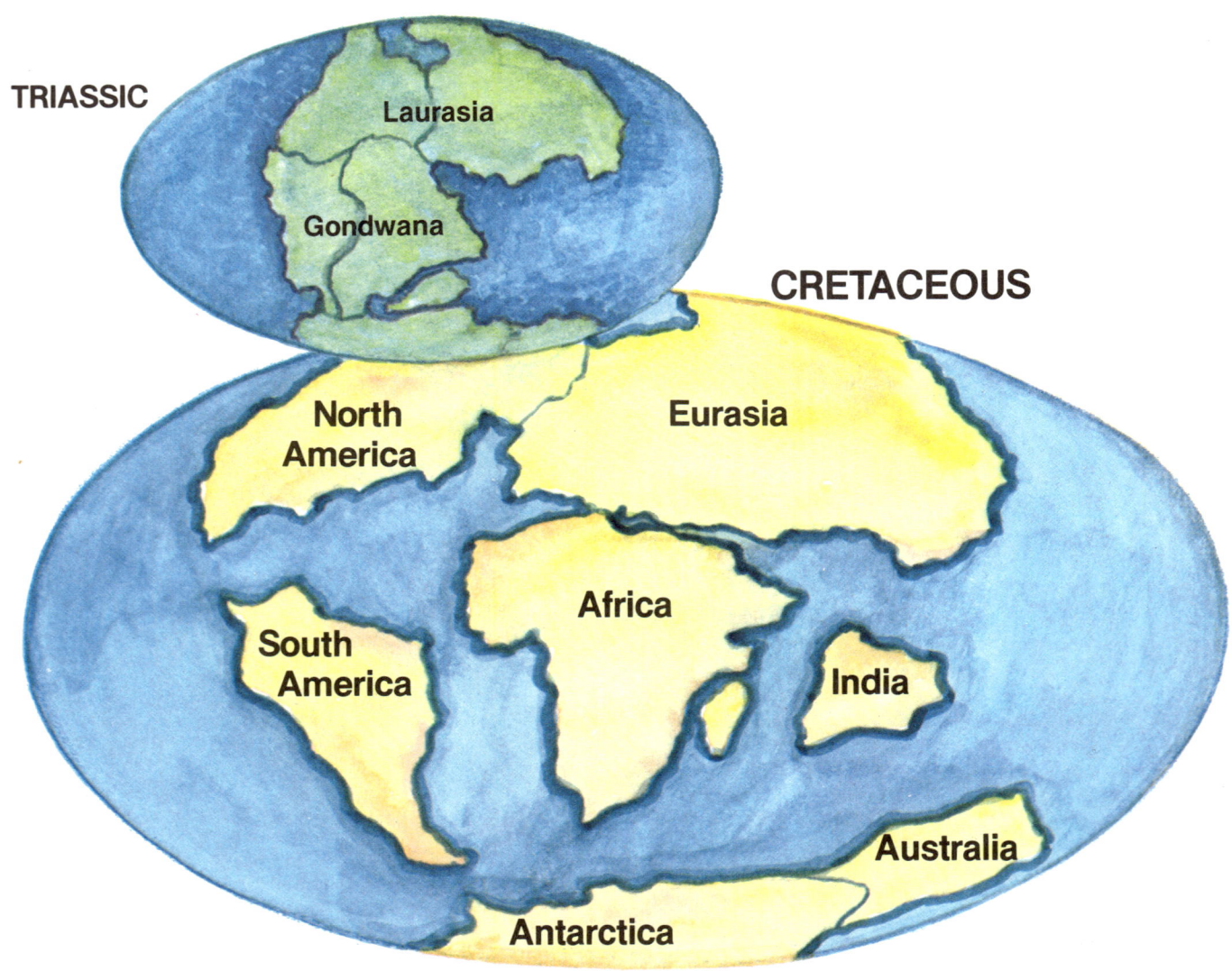

In the water were strange animals that looked like monsters. *Plesiosaurus* was one of these monsters.

The bodies of these sea animals were built for living in the water. Their legs were like flippers. These were helpful for swimming.

Although it breathed air, *Plesiosaurus* spent most of its time in the sea.

APPEARANCE

Plesiosaurus was about 10 feet (3 m) long and was one of the largest swimming reptiles. It weighed about 300 pounds (136 kg). It had a small head, with a large eye on each side. A nose was just in front of the eyes.

Plesiosaurus swam slowly on the top of the water. Its short paddle-like flippers moved it along, like turtles move. Scientists believe it could swim both forward and backward.

It may have used its flippers to crawl onto the sand, like a walrus does. The sandy beach was a good place on which to lay its eggs.

The long, snake-like neck bent easily and helped its head move around to look for food under water. *Plesiosaurus* ate small fish and other sea animals. When it saw a fish, it would stretch out its long neck. The strong jaws would quickly snap its sharp teeth over the fish.

MEAT-EATING ENEMIES

Plesiosaurus had to watch for other meat-eating, swimming reptiles. It paddled quickly to escape other swimming reptiles.

For example, *Mosasaurus* (mo´ suh sor´ uhs) could have crushed *Plesiosaurus*. Its jaws measured 4 feet (1.2 m) when open. It had very sharp teeth.

The largest swimming reptile of all, *Tylosaurus* (ti´ lo sor´ uhs), was 20 to 40 feet (6 to 12 m) long. It had a long, slim body. All the other sea animals would have tried to swim away from its sharp teeth.

CHAPTER 3: THE END OF PLESIOSAURUS

These swimming reptiles, including *Plesiosaurus,* died thousands of years ago, at the same time all the dinosaurs died. Paleontologists (pa´ le on tol´ uh jists) have many different ideas about why all the dinosaurs died.

Maybe the weather changed, and the air grew colder. Scientists are not sure what happened to change the weather.

Perhaps a big space rock, larger than 6 miles (10 km) across, hit the earth. Dust from the crash could have blocked out the sunlight, so the air would become cold.

It is possible that a star exploded in space and caused energy rays to kill the dinosaurs.

Maybe the dinosaurs became weak and died from a sickness.

Whatever happened, there were no more dinosaurs and no more swimming reptiles.

When these swimming reptiles died, their bodies sank to the bottom of the sea. Sand and mud covered the bodies, many of which turned into fossils. Thousands of years later, some of the fossils have now been found.

CONCLUSION: FOSSIL HUNTING TODAY

Fossils are found in different layers of rock. Scientists learn the age of fossils when they study the layer of rocks in which the fossils are found.

Scientists have learned that rock has the same layers in many parts of the earth. William Smith, a British scientist, reported this first.

Smith saw some rock layers that were made of mud. Other layers were made of sand, clay, dead plants, and dead animals. He made maps which showed more than thirty kinds of rock.

He had another idea. He thought that the oldest layers were on the bottom. Today, we know that this is not always true. Earthquakes have moved some older layers to the top.

"How wonderful that the fossils found by Mary Anning have helped scientists find so many other animal fossils!" Mychal exclaimed.

"Someday, I would like to find such great things. I want to begin to collect fossils of my own," he said.

MUSEUMS:

Here are some museums that have fossils of *Plesiosaurus*.

American Museum of Natural History, New York, NY.

Denver Museum of Natural History, Denver, CO.

National Museum of Natural History, Smithsonian Institution, Washington, DC. (*Plesiosaurus* exhibit expected to open soon.)

GLOSSARY:

CROCODILIANS (krok´ uh dil´ e uhnz) were reptiles that lived in the water. They looked a lot like crocodiles. The word is from the Greek **krokodelos,** which means "crocodile."

CYCAD (si´ kad) is a fern-like tree which lived many years ago.

DINOSAUR (di´ nuh sor´) means "terrible lizard." The Greek word **deinos** means "terrible," and the word **sauros** means "lizard."

ELASMOSAURUS (i laz´ muh sor´ uhs) was a long-necked plesiosaur that was about 43 feet (13 m) long and moved slowly with paddle-like flippers. The word is from the Greek **elasmos** which means "thin plate" and **sauros** which means "lizard."

EXHIBIT (ig zib´ it) refers to objects on display so people can see them.

FLIPPER (flip´ uhr) is a broad, flat limb, adapted for swimming.

FOSSILS (fos´ uhlz) are the remains of plants and animals that lived many years ago. The Latin word **fossilis** means "something dug up."

MOSASAURUS (mo´ suh sor´ uhs) was not a dinosaur. It was a horny, swimming lizard that looked like a sea dragon. Its name is from the Meuse River in Holland, where it was first found, plus the Greek word **sauros** which means "lizard."

MUSEUM (myoo ze´ uhm) is a place for keeping and exhibiting works of nature and art, scientific objects, and other items.

PALEONTOLOGIST (pa´ le on tol´ uh jist) is a person who studies fossils to learn about plants and animals from thousands of years ago. The Greek word **palaios** means "ancient," **onta** means "living things," and **logos** means "talking about."

PLESIOSAUR (ple´ se uh sor´) was the name for a group of swimming reptiles that lived thousands of years ago. They ate fish. They swam with flippers.

PLESIOSAUROIDS (ple´ se uh sor´ oids) were plesiosaurs that had long snaky necks, small heads, and bodies shaped like barrels. They swam near the top of the sea.

PLESIOSAURUS (ple´ se uh sor´ uhs) was an animal which was once thought to be related to the dinosaurs. The name means "near lizard." It comes from the Greek words **plesios** which means "near" and **sauros** which means "lizard."

PLIOSAUROIDS (pli´ uh sor´ oids) were plesiosaurs that were large, like whales, and had large heads with short necks. They dived into the sea to catch fish.

PTERODACTYLUS (ter´ uh dak´ til uhs) was a group of flying reptiles with long, curved necks and long faces. The name is from the Greek words **pteron** for "wing" and **daktylos** for "finger," because the fourth finger supported the wings.

REPTILES (rep´ tilz) are cold-blooded, egg-laying animals, such as snakes, alligators, and lizards. The legs grow out of the sides of the body, causing the reptile to crawl instead of walk. The Latin word **reptilis** means "creeping."

SCIENTIST (si´ uhn tist) is a person who studies objects or events.

SWEET GUM TREE (swet gum tre) is a large tree with shining, star-shaped leaves. It produces a balsam, used in making some chewing gum.

THOUSAND (thou´ zuhnd) is ten times one hundred. It is shown as 1,000.

TYLOSAURUS (ti´ lo sor´ uhs) was a large, meat-eating lizard that lived in the sea. It was 20 to 40 feet (6 to 12 m) long, with a slim body. It had sharp teeth and flipper-like legs. The word is from the Greek **tylos** which means "knot" and the word **sauros** which means "lizard."